SIDMOUTH

of Yesteryear

Chips Barber

D1513028

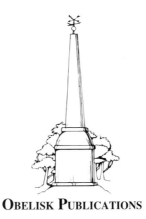

OBELISK PUBLICATIONS

OTHER TITLES IN THIS SERIES

St Thomas of Yesteryear, Parts I and II, *Mavis Piller*
Ashburton of Yesteryear, *John Germon and Pete Webb*
The Teign Valley of Yesteryear, Parts I and II, *Chips Barber*
Brixham of Yesteryear, Parts I, II and III, *Chips Barber*
Pinhoe of Yesteryear, Parts I and II, *Chips Barber*
Princetown of Yesteryear, Parts I and II, *Chips Barber*
Withycombe Raleigh of Yesteryear, Parts I and II, *Stocker/Gardner/Long/Southwell*
Kingsteignton of Yesteryear, *Richard Harris* • Ide of Yesteryear, *Mavis Piller*
Heavitree of Yesteryear, *Chips Barber* • Dawlish of Yesteryear, *Chips Barber*
Kenton and Starcross of Yesteryear, *Eric Vaughan*
Okehampton of Yesteryear, *Mike and Hilary Wreford*
Beesands and Hallsands of Yesteryear, *Cyril Courtney*
Exmouth of Yesteryear, *Kevin Palmer* • Littleham of Yesteryear, *Kevin Palmer*
Sampford Peverell of Yesteryear, *Bridget Bernhardt and Jenny Holley*
Whipton of Yesteryear, *Chips Barber and Don Lashbrook*
Kingskerswell of Yesteryear, *Chips Barber and John Hand*
Torquay of Yesteryear, *Leslie Retallick*
Lympstone of Yesteryear, *Anne Scott*
Whitchurch of Yesteryear, *Phil Maker* • Crediton of Yesteryear, *Victoria Labbett*
Chagford of Yesteryear, *Chips Barber* • Dartmoor of Yesteryear, *Chips Barber*
Burgh Island and Bigbury Bay of Yesteryear, *Chips Barber*
Devon's Railways of Yesteryear, *Chips Barber*
Exminster of Yesteryear, *Chips Barber* • Dartmouth of Yesteryear, *Chips Barber*

OTHER TITLES ABOUT THIS AREA

Sidmouth Past and Present, *Chips Barber*
Short Circular Walks in and around Sidmouth, *Chips Barber*
Walks on and around Woodbury Common, *Chips Barber*
Exmouth in Colour, *Chips Barber* • Along The Otter, *Chips Barber*
Topsham Past and Present, *Chips Barber* • Topsham in Colour, *Chips Barber*
Exmouth Century, Parts One and Two, *George Pridmore*
Entertaining Exmouth, *George Pridmore*
Exmouth to Starcross Ferry, *Harry Pascoe*
Strange Stories from Exmouth, *Tricia Gerrish*
Curiosities of East Devon, *Derrick Warren*
Around the Churches of East Devon, *Walter Jacobson*
Beer, *Chips Barber* • Branscombe, *Chips Barber*
Colyford and Colyton, *Chips Barber* • Seaton and Axmouth, *Chips Barber*

For a current list please send an SAE to
Obelisk Publications, 2 Church Hill, Pinhoe, Exeter EX4 9ER

Plate Acknowledgements

All pictures supplied by Barrie Hall

First published in 2001, reprinted in 2002 and 2006 by
Obelisk Publications, 2 Church Hill, Pinhoe, Exeter, Devon
Designed and Typeset by Sally Barber
Printed in Great Britain
by Avocet Press, Cullompton, Devon

© Obelisk Publications 2001

SIDMOUTH

of Yesteryear

This book is a photographic journey down the 'memory lane' of a Sidmouth of Yesteryear. If you study these fascinating picture postcard views – and the occasional photograph – from the amazing collection of Barrie Hall, you will see that although Sidmouth retains its elegant appearance, there have been many changes. I have covered more about Sidmouth's history in *Sidmouth Past & Present,* which will help to put these pictures into some sort of perspective.

As many people, in the past, arrived by train it is appropriate to start with the railway.

This small picture shows a train on the Sidmouth branch line in Harpford Woods. Having climbed steeply from Tipton St John it makes its way on towards the resort. The

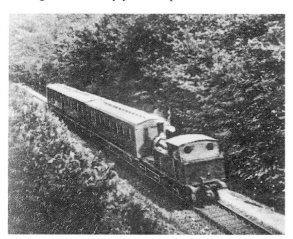

station in Sidmouth was quite a distance from the town and sea-front, and there were those who believed that this was deliberately done to deter 'trippers' – a walk of a mile or so to the beach and another one back at the end of a 'tiring day' by the sea would be enough to put off many day visitors. However, an examination of the lie of the land shows that from the former station towards the sea there is quite a slope, which would have been too steep for locomotives.

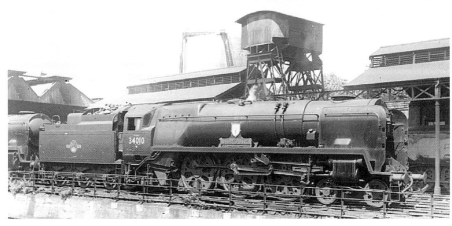

(Opposite) The station site has seen immense change in recent years and now bears little resemblance to how it looked in these pictures. The train at the bottom is called 'Sidmouth' and is shown here at Bournemouth. In recent times it has been renovated.

On this page we see the busy 'depot' of J. Lake & Son, Carriage Proprietors. They operated a flourishing delivery and people-conveying business and were delivery agents for the London & South Western Railway. Below is the seaward end of Station Road as it looked in about 1908. The card was sent from Warwick on 26 October of that year. Pebble Cottage can just about be seen beyond the people on the pavement. In those virtually traffic-free days it was also safe enough to walk in the road, or so it appears.

Above is the view from Peak Hill when Sidmouth looked a lot different. Jacob's Ladder, front right, is a straight up and down affair, and the house called 'Seaway' stands where the lovely Connaught Gardens are now located. Beyond the Sid there are scarcely any properties to be seen as fields spread over Salcombe Hill.

Below is the Clock Tower, now an attractive and fine place for refreshments or meals, and this has changed greatly in appearance since this picture was taken more than half a century ago. These colourful gardens were opened in 1934 by the Duke of Connaught, hence their name.

Jacob's Ladder is a popular place, as is shown in these three pictures. Note the changing facilities, a colony of tents providing the necessary 'seclusion' for donning beach apparel. The scene below is the oldest of the three, as there is no man-made terrace to be seen. All of these pictures were taken before the zig-zag chine, or walkway, which facilitates easier access to the beach for those who cannot cope with Jacob's Ladder, was built. For those who like trivia, Jacob's Ladder was featured in one of H. G. Wells' books, *The Sea Raiders*. Those who sit here have a grandstand view of the red sandstone coastline towards Ladram Bay and beyond.

The Victoria Hotel is certainly a fine establishment and one which has entertained many famous guests throughout the years. These include Sir Henry Wood, of the Promenade Concerts fame, and George Bernard Shaw, who, it is said, was 'beseiged' by adoring women fans. In order to escape their attentions it is believed that he had to make use of the fire escape! This long-established hotel is shown at the top of the view above and also in close-up below.

Above we have the 'new' and enlightened concept of 'mixed bathing'. At many places in Victorian and Edwardian times it was the norm to have segregated bathing areas and, invariably, the men got the beaches with the least, or no facilities. Where the tents are shown is now a walkway called Clifton Walk (opened in July 1999), named after the adjacent large cottages above it. It is now possible, sea conditions and tides permitting, to walk around to Jacob's Ladder, just beyond the bend.

Spot the differences? The picture above, with a 'downhill sea', is the older of the two, which are taken from almost the same place. It shows bathing machines on the beach, and a complete absence of cars or railings at this end of the resort. It must have been fairly quiet. The road looks to have had horses passing along it a little earlier! In the distance a paddle steamer can be seen at right angles to the beach. These were popular all along the south coast and, over a period of many years, hundreds of thousands of passengers enjoyed a bracing coastal cruise on the briny.

Below, the vehicular 'invasion' has begun, but motorists, it would appear, had the freedom to park almost anywhere they liked in the pre-yellow-lines and traffic-warden-free era. What bliss! The growing popularity of Sidmouth is also reflected in the substantial sea-front shelters which have appeared.

Above is the reverse view of the two opposite, looking back along the coastline towards High Peak and Ladram Bay. The Victorians here are protecting their heads from the heat of the noon-day sun, either with forms of headwear or parasols. At the water's edge a line of bathing machines can be seen.

Below, the hotel on the left is the Bedford Family Hotel with the name of the owner, John P. Millen, spelt out high on the side.

The Hotel Riviera is shown as a complete detached entity in the aerial shot below, but in the above picture the eastern end of this former terrace still looks like a number of separate houses. See how cleverly the doorways have been removed and how an extra storey has been incorporated at the expense of 'losing' the chimney pots.

Opposite are three shore scenes which reflect the moods of the sea. Sidmouth has often taken a battering from the sea and, consequently, its beach has often been eroded and its Esplanade damaged by storms. At other more benign times the beach has accumulated material.

Above are two 'old-timers', former Sidmouth fishermen Harry Bartlett and, on the right, 'Old Farrant'. Below is Theo Mortimore, who had an extremely loud voice, one which he put to good use, when travelling around the resort on his tricycle, by bawling out details of various events, arrivals, departures or incidents. If you wanted to make something known to a wider audience then Theo was your man. The expert ringing of his bell commanded the public's attention and his stentorian tones did the rest.

Some of these pictures are rare and therefore quite valuable. These two are such a pair and now command, at postcard fairs, a price many thousand times their original face value. They are date stamped, on the back, 20 March 1926, and mark the occasion when the Minister of Transport visited the resort when the reconstructed Esplanade was opened.

Visiting steamers were part of the seaside scene in the past. The vessels stationed themselves at a right angle to the beach and their passengers then had to 'walk the plank'. Perhaps the most famous vessel to call here was *The Duchess of Devonshire,* who unfortunately was beached here in the summer of 1934, as shown in the bottom right picture.

(Above) A tremendous crowd has gathered to see the hazardous launching of the Sidmouth Lifeboat. When it returned to 'port' a large team of horses had to be employed to pull it back up the beach. In 1912 the Lifeboat ceased to operate from Sidmouth and Exmouth, with its faster steam-powered boat, took over the responsibilities.

In the bottom picture, and opposite top, is Alma Bridge spanning the Sid, the river which gives its name to the resort.

Alma Bridge is named after a battle fought in 1854 during the Crimean War. It provides those who wish to walk the coastline towards Salcombe Regis and Branscombe with a dry passage. Beyond it the coast path, which used to skirt the cliff-edge, has fallen into the sea and a small inland diversion is now required.

Below is The Ham. In the Ham car park you can now find the swimming pool and the tourist information centre.

Not very far upstream from The Ham is a ford which is passable when the Sid is not in flood. Just about discernible, in the centre of the view, is the former toll-house at the end of the Byes. It doesn't need much detective work to see which is the older of these two similar scenes. The one below was posted on 14 September 1923 for a penny, exactly twice the amount it cost to send the one above. What a price hike!

Opposite are two views taken in opposite directions. The top picture looks up Salcombe Road whilst the one below shows the sharp bend in the road near the toll-house. Although both scenes have changed somewhat they are still instantly recognisable.

The same may be said of these two views, which show both sides of Salcombe Road. The best way to appreciate the changes is to take this book along to the point where they were taken and then compare the differences 'in the field'.

Opposite are three different places. (Top) The Knowle Hotel is now the headquarters of East Devon District Council. (Middle) Bickwell Valley is recognisable although the road which runs along it is less 'countrified' than when this shot was taken a century ago. (Bottom) This picture shows the Old Chancel and one is most unlikely to see cattle there today!

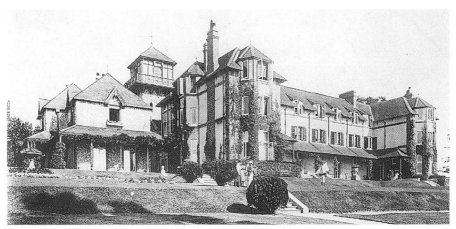

Here is a 'before and after' view of part of Church Street, one of the most attractive streets in the resort. The top picture is before 12 December 1927 and the bottom is after that fateful day. The top right and bottom pictures opposite were taken that day, when a great fire accounted for the buildings which originally stood on the site. Sidmouth has, unfortunately, suffered several major blazes. Top left shows Clifton Cottage, near the Victoria Hotel, well alight.

The view above is Prospect Place, the building on the far right being the Mocha restaurant. The building on the extreme left is the Marlborough Hotel, now a place where, in fine weather, brightly coloured umbrellas or parasols add a splash of colour to the street scene.

Below is Fore Street, and there isn't a single large lorry to obstruct the flow of traffic. Halcyon days!

Above is Sidmouth Market in the days when there was only one telephone box and part-pedestrianised schemes were unnecessary. The middle picture shows the parting of the ways between Fore Street and Old Fore Street with cars parked facing in both directions. Can you imagine what this 'thoroughfare' would be like now with two-way traffic? Below, there is no traffic problem in the High Street as horse and carts ply up or down it. Despite the passing of a great many years, the scene hasn't changed enormously although the 'personnel' are now different.

The postcard above was sent to Miss Edwards of 63 Lansdown Road, Canton, Cardiff, on 15 June 1906. The view is taken in the High Street. I'll leave the bottom one for you to discover where it was taken, it's more fun that way … The arrangement of windows should help.

There was quite a gathering for the opening, on 17 September 1906, of the Mill Street premises of the Co-op. Below is the bus which ran between Salcombe Hill and Peak Hill. After its working life in the resort it went to Bicton Gardens, where it continued to give people rides around the park. The middle picture is of the former Connaught School, which later became the Liberal Hall but is now converted to shops.

The name 'Ellis' appears on both these cards and this fine photographer was responsible for many included in this book. He was a man who would move as soon as he 'caught wind' of something happening in Sidmouth and was always there for the 'action'. Above is one of his more passive pictures, but the one below shows quite a gathering near the club house of the golf course.

There is, just to the left of the lamp-post, a small cross marked on the edge of the pavement. The significance of this 'addition' to Jubilee Terrace, in All Saints Road, is that the sender stayed there and posted this card on 18 October 1916. He noted the unseasonal weather when he wrote, 'It has been lovely, hot and sunny. I sat on the front in the sun all morning.' Below is another rare card, this time showing a view of Peasland Road when it had some young trees growing at the edge of the pavements on either side. This card was posted on 26 August 1910, which gives us an approximate date for when the picture was taken. It was common then to include residential streets as postcard views, probably because householders, without telephones, faxes or e-mails, used them to send messages. Local ones often had same-day delivery!

The lower regions of Sidmouth have always been prone to flooding. When such inundations occur there is always someone ready, willing and able to man the boats in order to make an unusual photo! The picture above, showing the cinema, was taken in 1924 and the one below is from 1960, a year notorious for its floods around Devon.

And on that watery note we end this sequence of pictures, which shows the resort in its sedate and also its more saturated moments.